D1661616

Note: This journal is not a substitute for therapy with a licensed professional. If you need the help of a professional, please seek the services of a licensed provider.

We are very grateful for your support on this project <3

If you like the journal and you think it can bring you something good, you would help us a lot by leaving a review on Amazon to reach many more people like you and make the project grow.

¡Thank you!

Introduction: Embracing Mindfulness

Are you ready to embark on your mindfulness and meditation journey? Let's dive in together! As you embark on this journey through the art of mindfulness, envision these words as a comforting hug, a whispered reassurance that you are not alone on this path to inner peace.

In this sacred space, my intention is not to inundate you with facts or overwhelm you with information. Instead, picture me as a trusted friend inviting you to sit for a while, sharing stories that resonate with the beating of your heart. This book is more than a guide; it is a companion on your quest for tranquility.

A Personal Anecdote: A Whisper from My Own Journey

Allow me to share a piece of my own soul's journey with mindfulness, a journey not void of trials and tribulations. There was a time when life felt like a stormy sea, tossing me amidst its waves of responsibilities, expectations, and uncertainties. It was amidst this chaos that I stumbled upon the sanctuary of mindfulness.

In the gentle rhythm of my breath, I found solace. Each inhale became a moment of self-discovery, and each exhale a release of burdens carried for far too long. It was not a miraculous transformation but a gradual unfolding—a tender unfurling of petals in the sunlight of awareness.

Through my experiences, I discovered the transformative power of mindfulness, not as a rigid discipline but as a compassionate friend holding my hand through life's twists and turns. It became a sanctuary where I could return to myself, time and again, to find peace amid life's beautiful chaos.

Our Shared Purpose: A Supportive Guide to Inner Peace

As we embark on this shared odyssey, know that my aim is not to instruct but to nurture. This book is a testament to the belief that within the folds of mindfulness lies a sanctuary waiting to be discovered by every weary heart. Whether you are a novice seeking solace or a seasoned traveler on the path, these pages are a haven for you.

Here, you'll find a gentle guide, filled not only with practices but with the warmth of understanding. Together, we will explore the essence of mindfulness—a practice not of perfection but of presence. It is my sincere hope that you feel the supportive embrace of these words, encouraging you to cultivate your own inner garden of serenity.

May this journey be as much about self-compassion as it is about mindfulness, and may you find, within these pages, the gentle encouragement needed to unfold the petals of your own inner peace.

Peace comes from within.
Do not seek it without.

- Buddha

Chapter 1: The Heart of Mindfulness

Welcome, awesome reader, to the heart of our exploration—mindfulness, a sanctuary where compassion and self-acceptance intertwine, creating a tapestry of healing and inner peace.

Defining Mindfulness: A Compassionate Presence

Mindfulness is more than a mere practice; it is an art, a way of being in the world with a gentle and open heart. Picture it as the soft light that illuminates the darkest corners of our minds, inviting us to see ourselves with kindness and understanding. Mindfulness, in its essence, is the art of being present, of turning our attention to the current moment without judgment.

But it's not just about being present; it's about being present with kindness. In the gentle embrace of mindfulness, we learn to hold our experiences with compassion, as a nurturing mother cradles her child. It's an invitation to witness our thoughts, emotions, and sensations without criticism, allowing them to unfold like delicate petals in the sunlight of acceptance.

The Caring Nature of Mindfulness: A Balm for the Soul

At the core of mindfulness lies a profound compassion—a caring gaze turned inward. It's about creating a space within ourselves where our struggles are acknowledged with tenderness, where our imperfections are not blemishes but unique brushstrokes in the canvas of our existence.

Consider mindfulness as the warm cup of tea offered to a friend in distress, a comforting presence in times of joy and sorrow alike. This practice is not a stern teacher pointing out flaws but a gentle guide, encouraging you to explore the vast landscapes of your inner world with a heart full of kindness.

As we delve into the heart of mindfulness, let us embark on a journey of self-discovery, where each breath is an opportunity to nurture the garden of our souls. Together, we'll uncover the power of mindfulness not only as a tool for awareness but as a source of solace, an ever-present friend offering compassion on the path to self-acceptance.

In the gentle heart of mindfulness, we embark on a journey woven with compassion and self-acceptance, discovering the transformative power of our breath. Let's explore a few breathing exercises together—a comforting invitation to the sanctuary of the present moment.

Loving Kindness Breath: Nurturing the Heart

As you find a cozy seat, close your eyes, and take a moment to breathe deeply. Imagine with each inhalation a tender light entering your being—warm and loving. On the exhale, share this gentle light first with yourself, embracing your essence with kindness. Inhale once more, extending this luminous warmth to someone dear to you. Allow the circle of compassion to expand, reaching acquaintances, strangers, and those who may challenge you. Conclude by bringing this compassionate light back to your own heart, recognizing your deserving spirit.

Gratitude Breath: A Symphony of Thankfulness

Sit comfortably, breathe deeply, and let your mind dwell on gratitude. Inhale gratitude for a specific moment, and with each exhale, release tension. Continue this rhythmic dance, allowing each breath to unveil a new facet of your life to be grateful for—big or small. With every inhalation, let gratitude fill your heart; with every exhalation, release any lingering negativity. Take a moment at the end to appreciate the sensations and emotions that have blossomed during this practice.

Mindful Breath Counting: Anchoring the Present

Sit with grace, your back straight, and shoulders at ease. Inhale deeply, silently counting "one" in your mind. Exhale slowly and completely. Continue this pattern, counting each inhalation until you reach ten. If your thoughts wander, gently guide them back to the counting, free from judgment. After reaching ten, start anew. This simple practice of mindful breath counting enhances focus and concentration—a gentle anchor in the sea of the present moment.

Celebrity Quotes about Meditation and Mindfulness

Here are some famous celebrities who have openly discussed their experiences with meditation and mindfulness, along with snippets of what they have shared:

- Oprah Winfrey:

  - *"I walked out of that meditation, and I'll tell you, I was shocked. I was in a state of such stillness that it was hard for me to comprehend."*

- Ellen DeGeneres:

  - *"I started meditating a few years ago, and I've been doing TM (Transcendental Meditation) regularly ever since. When I do it regu-*

larly, I just feel like I can handle anything that comes up. It just gives me this peaceful feeling."

- Kobe Bryant:
  - *"Meditation for me means I can start the day off with a positive mindset. It's helped me to become a better person, a calmer person, and it's changed my life."*

- Jennifer Aniston:
  - *"I started being a little bit more mindful, and yoga helps with that. I love it. I have a lot of friends who do Transcendental Meditation, and I enjoy a 20-minute sit down at the end of the day."*

These quotes highlight how meditation and mindfulness have made a positive impact on these celebrities' lives, fostering a sense of calm, clarity, and resilience.

Dear reader, as we engage in these exercises, let them be more than steps to follow but an invitation to a mindful dance, a caring exploration of the profound nature of your breath—the heartbeat of mindfulness. In each inhale and exhale, may you discover the gentle embrace of self-compassion and acceptance.

Chapter 2: The Gentle Power of Breath

Greetings, mindful adventurer, to the enchanting realm of mindful breathing—an artful dance with the breath, where the simple act of inhaling and exhaling unveils profound transformations. In this chapter, let us explore the tender embrace of the breath, a gentle force that holds the key to inner serenity.

Introducing the Transformative Power:
A Dance with the Breath

Picture the breath as your loyal companion, always present, offering a gentle rhythm to the song of your life. In the heart of mindful breathing lies a transformative power—a quiet force capable of soothing the turbulence within. It is more than just the exchange of air; it is a pathway to presence, a portal to the calm sanctuary that resides within each inhalation and exhalation.

As we embark on this exploration, envision your breath as a delicate dance—a waltz of the present moment. With each inhalation, you draw in the essence of now, and with each exhale, you release what no longer serves you. In this dance, you'll find the magic of mindfulness, unfolding like petals in the soft breeze of your breath.

Simple Breathing Exercises: Nurturing the Dance Within

Let us embark on a journey of nurturing breath exercises, simple yet profound, inviting you to become acquainted with the gentle power within you:

1. Soothing Waves Breath:

Inhale slowly, imagining the breath as a gentle wave caressing the shore.

Exhale with equal grace, feeling the wave recede.

Repeat, allowing each breath to wash away tension and welcome tranquility.

2. Heart-Centered Breath:

Place your hand over your heart.

Inhale, feeling the expansion of your chest beneath your hand.

Exhale, sensing the gentle contraction.

Let each breath radiate warmth and compassion from your heart.

3. Candle Flame Breath:

Picture a tiny, flickering candle flame in your mind.

Inhale, envisioning the flame growing brighter.

Exhale, watching it gently sway.

Feel the calming energy of the flame with each breath.

Stories of Solace: Whispered Testimonies

Within the pages of this chapter, you'll find stories—whispers from souls who discovered solace in mindful breathing. Meet Sarah, who found calm in the rhythmic dance of her breath during moments of anxiety. Explore the journey of Mark, who, through mindful breathing, learned to navigate the currents of stress with grace.

These stories are not just anecdotes; they are testimonials to the gentle power of breath, illustrating how the simple act of turning inward and embracing the breath can be a source of profound comfort and resilience. As you engage with these narratives, may you feel the nurturing embrace of mindful breathing, whispering the promise of tranquility in every inhalation and exhalation.

Sarah's Journey: Finding Calm Amidst Chaos

In the hustle and bustle of Sarah's daily life, anxiety often knocked on her door like an uninvited guest. The demands of work and the relentless pace of modern living left her feeling overwhelmed. One day, amidst the storm of stress, Sarah discovered the gentle power of mindful breathing.

In the quiet moments, she would close her eyes, grounding herself in the present. With each inhalation, she visualized a calming wave washing over her, and with each exhale, she released the tension that clung to her like heavy mist. The rhythm of her breath became a sanctuary, a soothing melody that drowned out the noise of anxiety.

As days turned into weeks, Sarah noticed a subtle shift. The once frenetic pace of her thoughts slowed down, and the waves of anxiety began to ebb away. Mindful breathing became her anchor, a reliable friend she could turn to in moments of turmoil. Through the gentle dance of her breath, Sarah found a haven of calmness within, a place where serenity awaited her, ready to embrace her with open arms.

Mark's Tale: Navigating Stress with Grace

Mark, a diligent professional with a demanding career, often found himself caught in the whirlwind of stress. The pressures of deadlines and the weight of responsibilities created a constant hum of tension in his life. In the midst of this chaos, Mark discovered the transformative potential of mindful breathing.

During high-stakes meetings or moments of intense pressure, Mark would pause, allowing his breath to become the focal point. Inhaling deeply, he imagined the expansion of his chest as a symbolic release of stress, and as he exhaled, he visualized the stress dissipating like a dissipating fog. Through this rhythmic dance of breath, Mark found a profound sense of clarity and composure.

With time, mindful breathing became Mark's secret weapon against stress. It was not about eliminating challenges but about facing them with grace and resilience. The simple yet powerful act of breathing mindfully allowed him to navigate the currents of stress with a new-found sense of poise.

Sarah and Mark's stories are testaments to the transformative nature of mindful breathing. Their experiences remind us that amidst life's challenges, the breath can be a steadfast companion—a source of solace and strength. As you engage with these narratives, may you find inspiration in the journeys of others and discover the profound impact that mindful breathing can have on your own path to inner peace.

Examples of Celebrities:

Celebrities Unveiling the Power of Breath

In the glittering realm of fame and stardom, where the spotlight never dims, even the brightest stars face moments of stress and pressure. Yet, amidst the chaos, some celebrities have discovered a secret weapon that transcends the red carpets and adoring fans—the simple power of breath. In this exploration, we delve into the lives of three iconic figures who have openly embraced breathing exercises as a means to navigate the turbulent seas of their demanding careers. Join us as we uncover the intimate stories of how Hugh Jackman, Emma Watson, and LeBron James harness the ancient wisdom of mindful breathing to find calm amid the storms of their extraordinary lives. These are not just tales of celebrity rituals; they are whispers of resilience, proving that, no matter the stage, the ability to breathe mindfully is a universal key to tranquility and triumph.

- Hugh Jackman:

  - Known for his roles in blockbuster films, has openly shared his practice of mindfulness and breathing exercises to manage stress. He emphasizes the importance of conscious breathing in staying centered and focused, especially in high-pressure situations.

- Emma Watson:

- Actress and activist Emma Watson has spoken about incorporating mindfulness and breathing techniques into her daily routine. She credits these practices for helping her maintain balance, clarity, and resilience amid the demands of her career and public life.

- LeBron James:

- NBA superstar LeBron James has been vocal about using breathing exercises to stay calm and focused during intense moments on the basketball court. He incorporates mindfulness techniques, including controlled breathing, as part of his mental preparation for games, contributing to his overall performance and well-being.

Chapter 3: Cultivating Self-Compassion

As we delve into the tender terrain of self-compassion—a radiant garden within the landscape of mindfulness. In this chapter, we embark on a journey of embracing ourselves with the warmth and kindness we readily extend to others.

Exploring Self-Compassion: A Gentle Unveiling

Imagine self-compassion as the gentle rain that nurtures the blossoms of your soul. It's an art—a way of relating to yourself with a soft heart, especially in moments of challenge or vulnerability. In mindfulness, self-compassion is not a luxury but an essential companion, a balm for the inevitable bumps on our journey.

Let us unfold the layers of self-compassion, recognizing that it's more than forgiveness; it's an acknowledgment of our shared humanity. It's an embrace that whispers, "You are not alone in your struggles; we all stumble, and that's okay."

Exercises in Kindness: Nurturing Your Inner Sanctuary

1. Loving-Kindness Meditation:
Find a comfortable position and close your eyes.
Inhale deeply, and with each exhale, extend wishes of well-being to yourself.

Gradually expand these wishes to others—loved ones, acquaintances, even those you may find challenging. Conclude by returning these wishes to yourself, recognizing your own deserving spirit.

2. The Compassionate Letter:

Write a letter to yourself as you would to a dear friend facing a challenge. Acknowledge your struggles with kindness and offer words of encouragement. Read the letter with a compassionate heart, recognizing the shared human experience.

3. Self-Compassion Break:

In moments of difficulty, pause and acknowledge your feelings. Remind yourself that challenges are a part of life shared by all. Place a hand on your heart and offer words of comfort, such as "May I be kind to myself in this moment."

Personal Reflections: A Mirror of Compassion

In the tapestry of my own journey, self-compassion has been a gentle companion. There were moments when I stumbled and felt the weight of self-judgment. Yet, through the practice of mindfulness, I learned to embrace my imperfections with tenderness.

Self-compassion is not about perfection but about meeting ourselves with an open heart. It's a daily practice of acknowledging our humanity, celebrating our strengths, and cradling our vulnerabilities. In these reflections, may you find echoes of your own journey, recognizing that the path to self-compassion is a shared pilgrimage.

As we navigate this chapter together, let the exercises be whispers of kindness, guiding you to cultivate a relationship with yourself that mirrors the warmth and care you naturally extend to others. May you embark on this journey of self-compassion with a heart brimming with love and understanding.

Guided Meditations: A Tapestry of Inner Kindness

As we continue our exploration of self-compassion, let us delve into the realm of guided meditations—a sacred offering to weave threads of kindness, relaxation, gratitude, and self-compassion into the fabric of your being. Whether in the form of soothing audio recordings or carefully crafted written instructions, these guided meditations are an invitation to a sanctuary within.

1. Relaxation Meditation: Finding Calm Within

Audio Recording:
Find a comfortable space and press play on the guided relaxation

meditation. Close your eyes and let the soothing voice guide you through a journey of releasing tension. Visualize each breath as a gentle wave, washing away stress and leaving tranquility in its wake.

Written Instructions:

Sit or lie down in a comfortable position.

Inhale deeply, allowing your breath to fill your lungs.

As you exhale, release any tension in your body, starting from your toes and gradually moving up. Continue this process, bringing awareness to each part of your body, until you reach a state of complete relaxation.

2. Gratitude Meditation: Nurturing the Heart

Audio Recording:

Press play on the gratitude meditation and allow the guide's words to lead you into a space of appreciation. Visualize moments and people for whom you are grateful, feeling the warmth of gratitude expanding within you. Embrace the positive emotions that arise, cultivating a grateful heart.

Written Instructions:

Sit comfortably and close your eyes. Begin by reflecting on three things you are grateful for today. With each item, take a moment to savor the feelings of gratitude, allowing them to permeate your being. Expand your focus to include a broader range of blessings, feeling a sense of thankfulness for the richness of your life.

3. *Self-Compassion Meditation: Embracing Your Essence*

Audio Recording:
Allow the self-compassion meditation to envelop you in a cocoon of gentle words. Follow the guide's prompts to offer yourself words of kindness and understanding. Embrace any emotions that arise with an open heart, recognizing the beauty of self-compassion.

Written Instructions:
Find a quiet space and sit with a posture of ease.
Inhale deeply, acknowledging any challenges or struggles you may be facing. Exhale, offering yourself words of comfort and compassion. Repeat phrases such as "May I be kind to myself" and "I am deserving of love and understanding."

4. *Goal Visualization Meditation: Painting Your Future Canvas*

Audio Recording:
Immerse yourself in the guided meditation for goal visualization.

Envision your goals coming to life as the guide leads you through a vivid exploration of your desired future. Feel the emotions associated with your achievements, anchoring them in the present moment.

Written Instructions:

Sit in a quiet space and close your eyes. Picture your goals as if they have already been achieved. Engage your senses—feel the textures, hear the sounds, and immerse yourself in the details. Allow the positive emotions to resonate within you, fostering a sense of motivation and determination.

Dear reader, these guided meditations are offerings of self-care, each a brushstroke on the canvas of your inner world. Whether you choose to listen to the soothing voice of a guide or follow written instructions, may these meditations be gentle companions on your journey to self-compassion. As you breathe through each moment, may you find solace, gratitude, and a deep sense of kindness within.

Body Scan Exercises: A Symphony of Self-Discovery

As we navigate the chapters of self-compassion, let us introduce a practice that invites you to embark on a conscious journey through your own being—the body scan exercise. This gentle exploration serves as a compass, guiding you to areas of tension, inviting release, and fostering a deeper connection with both your physical and emotional landscapes.

The Body as a Sanctuary: An Introduction to Body Scan

Imagine your body as a sacred temple, a vessel that holds the stories of your experiences, joys, and challenges. The body scan exercise is an opportunity to visit each room of this temple with a mindful and caring presence, acknowledging the whispers of both physical and emotional sensations.

How to Engage in a Body Scan: A Step-by-Step Guide

1. Prepare the Space:
Find a quiet and comfortable place to sit or lie down.
Allow your body to settle into a position that feels supportive.

2. Begin with Breath:
Close your eyes and take a few deep breaths to center yourself.
Feel the gentle rise and fall of your chest with each inhalation and exhalation.

3. Directing Attention:

Start by bringing your awareness to the top of your head.

Slowly scan down through your body, part by part, or in whatever order feels natural to you.

4. Notice Sensations:

As you focus on each area, pay attention to any sensations you encounter—warmth, coolness, tension, or relaxation.

Be curious about the nuances of your body's messages.

5. Acknowledging Without Judgment:

When you encounter areas of tension or discomfort, approach them with a gentle curiosity.

Acknowledge these sensations without judgment, as if you were comforting a dear friend.

6. Allowing Release:

With each exhale, visualize releasing any tension or stress you identify.

Imagine your breath carrying away any burdens, leaving a sense of spaciousness and ease.

7. Closing with Gratitude:

Conclude the body scan by expressing gratitude for the wisdom and resilience your body holds.

Take a few moments to appreciate the journey you've just undertaken.

Encouragement for the Reader: A Message of Self-Care

Dear reader, as you engage in the body scan exercise, let it be a practice of self-love and care. Your body is a remarkable ally, and this exercise is an invitation to listen to its whispers, to recognize the areas where it may be holding onto stress or tension. Through this intentional exploration, may you discover the intricate dance between your physical and emotional well-being.

Remember, there is no rush in this journey. Allow the body scan to unfold at its own pace, honoring the sensations that arise without judgment. As you traverse the landscape of your body, may you find not only areas of tension but also reservoirs of strength and resilience. This exercise is an act of kindness—a gift you offer to yourself.

Chapter 4: Embracing the Present Moment

Hello, kindred spirit, as we wander into the enchanting realm of the present—a place where the beauty of life unfolds in every fleeting moment. In this chapter, we embark on a journey of mindful living, a celebration of the simple yet profound moments that weave the tapestry of our existence.

The Beauty of the Present Moment: A Symphony of Now

Consider, for a moment, the exquisite beauty of the present. It is not just a point in time but a vibrant tapestry woven with the threads of sights, sounds, and sensations. Living in the present is like sipping from the cup of life, relishing each sip with a heart brimming with gratitude.

Let us open our hearts to the beauty that surrounds us—the warmth of sunlight on our skin, the melody of birdsong, the gentle rustle of leaves in the breeze. The present moment is a canvas waiting to be painted with the hues of our awareness.

Practical Tips for Mindful Living: Nurturing the Now

1. Breath as an Anchor:
In moments of busyness, pause and take a few mindful breaths.

Feel the rise and fall of your chest, grounding yourself in the present moment.

2. *Mindful Walking:*

Whether indoors or outdoors, savor the act of walking. Feel the sensation of each step, the connection between your feet and the ground.

3. *Mindful Eating:*

Engage your senses during meals—notice the colors, textures, and flavors. Take a moment to express gratitude for the nourishment before you.

4. *Digital Detox:*

Dedicate specific times of the day for a digital detox. Allow yourself to be fully present without the distractions of screens.

5. *Five Senses Check-In:*

Take a moment to check in with each of your five senses.
What do you see, hear, smell, taste, and feel in this moment?

Stories of Joy in Simplicity: A Tapestry of Moments

Let me share with you the story of Emma, a woman whose heart found joy in the simplest moments. In the midst of a hectic work-day, Emma would take a mindful pause. She would step outside, feel the breeze on her face, and take a few deep breaths. In these stolen moments, she found a wellspring of joy that fueled her spirit for the tasks ahead.

And then there's Lily, who discovered the beauty of mindful eating. In each bite, she embraced the richness of flavors, savoring the textures and expressions of gratitude for the nourishment she provided to her body.

These stories are not extraordinary tales but whispers of the extraordinary in the ordinary. They remind us that joy is not reserved for grand occasions but is woven into the fabric of our daily lives. As you embrace the present moment, may you find your own stories of joy, each one a precious gem in the necklace of your existence.

Dear reader, let the practical tips and stories within these pages be your companions on the journey of mindful living. In the embrace of the present moment, may you discover a wellspring of joy and a sanctuary of peace.

Mindfulness Practices in Daily Life: Nurturing the Tapestry of Now

As we continue our exploration of embracing the present moment, let us unfurl the wings of mindfulness into the vast landscape of our daily lives. These are not separate moments reserved for meditation cushions; rather, they are opportunities to infuse every heartbeat with the grace of awareness. Here, we invite mindfulness to dance with us in the ordinary, transforming routine into ritual.

1. Mindful Eating: Savoring the Symphony of Flavors

Imagine your meals as a feast for the senses, a celebration of nourishment that extends beyond the physical. Engage in mindful eating by:

- Setting the Scene: Create a calm atmosphere for your meals. Light a candle, play soft music, or enjoy your food in a peaceful setting.

- Sensory Awareness: Before taking a bite, notice the colors, textures, and smells of your food.

- Chew with Intention: Take your time with each bite, savoring the flavors and textures. Put your utensils down between bites to cultivate a more mindful pace.

2. Mindful Walking: A Journey into the Present

Transform your daily walks into a mindful pilgrimage, each step a celebration of the present moment. Try:

- Conscious Footsteps: As you walk, pay attention to the sensation of each step. Feel the ground beneath you and the gentle sway of your body in motion.

- Breathing with Each Step: Sync your breath with your steps. Inhale for a few steps, exhale for a few more. Let your breath guide the rhythm of your walk.

- Nature Appreciation: If possible, walk in nature. Notice the colors, scents, and sounds around you. Let the beauty of your surroundings become a focal point.

3. Mindfulness in Chores: Transforming the Mundane into the Sacred

Household chores need not be a mundane task but an opportunity for mindfulness to unfold. Consider:

- Conscious Cleaning: Whether washing dishes or sweeping the floor, bring your full attention to the task at hand. Notice the sensations and movements involved.

- Sensory Engagement: Engage your senses by paying attention to the textures, scents, and sounds associated with your chores. Feel the water on your hands or the warmth of a freshly cleaned surface.

- Gratitude for Maintenance: Shift your perspective from viewing chores as burdens to recognizing them as acts of care for your living space.

4. Mindfulness in Interactions: Present in Connection

Extend mindfulness to your interactions with others. In conversations:

- Listen with Presence: Truly listen to the words spoken, without formulating your response while the other person talks.

- Pause Before Responding: Take a moment before replying, allowing your words to arise from a place of mindfulness rather than reactive impulse.

- Eye Contact and Presence: Make eye contact during conversations, expressing your engagement and connection.

Dear reader, as you weave mindfulness into the fabric of your daily activities, may each moment become an opportunity for presence. These practices are not burdens but gifts—a conscious choice to infuse your life with the richness of awareness. In the sacred dance of daily rituals, may you find joy, peace, and a profound connection to the symphony of now.

Chapter 5: Navigating Challenges with Grace

Welcome back, dear friend, as we venture into the heart of mindfulness—a sacred journey that, like any path, may be met with challenges. In this chapter, we shall navigate these challenges with grace, guided by the compassionate light within, acknowledging that the twists and turns are part of the transformative dance.

Acknowledging Common Challenges: A Compassionate Recognition

In the tapestry of mindfulness, challenges are threads woven into the fabric of growth. Let us acknowledge some common companions on this journey:

1. Restless Mind: The flutter of thoughts, like butterflies, can distract us from the present moment.

2. Impatience: The desire for instant results, a gentle nudging reminder that transformation unfolds in its own time.

3. Physical Discomfort: The body, a faithful companion, may protest against the stillness, inviting us to explore the balance between comfort and discomfort.

4. Self-Judgment: The echoes of self-criticism, a conditioned re-

sponse that may arise when faced with perceived shortcomings in our practice.

Guidance with Compassion: Nurturing Your Inner Garden

In the face of these challenges, let us cultivate a garden of compassion. Like a skilled gardener tending to delicate blossoms, we can navigate the hurdles with tender care:

1. Restless Mind: The Dance of Thoughts

Gently acknowledge the thoughts without judgment. Picture them as clouds passing through the vast sky of your mind. Redirect your focus to the breath, grounding yourself in the present moment.

2. Impatience: A Lesson in Patience

Embrace patience as a guiding companion. The journey of mindfulness is a gradual unfolding, not a destination to be rushed towards. Celebrate small victories and progress, savoring the subtle shifts in your awareness.

3. Physical Discomfort: Listening to the Body

Approach discomfort with curiosity. Where does it manifest, and how does it evolve? Adjust your posture mindfully or introduce gentle movements to alleviate tension.

4. Self-Judgment: Cultivating Self-Compassion

When self-judgment arises, meet it with kindness. Imagine offering yourself the same comforting words you would share with a dear friend facing similar challenges. Recognize that the path of mindfulness is not about perfection but about the journey of self-discovery.

Stories of Triumph Over Challenges: Whispers of Resilience

Let me share with you the stories of two remarkable individuals—Emily and Sophia—whose journeys embraced and transcended challenges through the lens of mindfulness.

Emily's Triumph Over Restlessness:
Emily, initially troubled by a restless mind, found solace in the metaphor of a flowing river. Each thought became a leaf gently floating downstream. With this perspective, she learned to witness her thoughts without feeling entangled by them.

Sophia's Dance with Impatience:
Sophia, a fervent seeker of immediate results, discovered the power of mindful reflection. Through journaling her experiences, she recognized the subtle transformations occurring over time. This revelation allowed her to release the grip of impatience and trust the

unfolding process.

Here are a few examples of celebrities who have overcome challenges and demonstrated resilience:

- *Dwayne "The Rock" Johnson:*

  - Before becoming a Hollywood star, Dwayne Johnson experienced multiple setbacks, including a failed football career and a period of depression. He turned his life around through hard work and resilience, emerging as a successful actor and entrepreneur.

- *J.K. Rowling:*

  - J.K. Rowling, the author of the Harry Potter series, faced rejection from multiple publishers before finding success. She overcame personal struggles and financial hardships, proving that resilience can lead to extraordinary achievements.

- *Michael Jordan:*

  - Widely regarded as one of the greatest basketball players of all time, Michael Jordan faced numerous setbacks, including being cut from his high school basketball team. His resilience and determination led him to multiple NBA championships and global success.

- Serena Williams:

- Serena Williams, a tennis legend, overcame health challenges and criticism throughout her career. Despite facing setbacks, she continues to dominate the tennis world and inspire others with her resilience.

These celebrities' stories serve as whispers of resilience, reminding us that challenges can be stepping stones to success.

Dear reader, may these stories be lanterns guiding you through the challenges that may arise on your path. In the garden of mindfulness, challenges are not obstacles but opportunities for growth. As you navigate the twists and turns, may you embrace each step with grace, recognizing that the journey is a dance, and every misstep is a gentle reminder to return to the rhythm of your breath.

As we conclude our exploration of navigating challenges with grace, we now embark on a profound journey of self-reflection—a sanctuary where honesty and vulnerability coalesce. Just as the challenges we discussed are threads woven into the fabric of our growth, these questions are lanterns guiding us through the corridors of our inner landscapes. In this sacred space, we shall unveil the layers of our being with tenderness and curiosity. Each question is an invitation to delve deeper into the tapestry of our experiences, embracing the complexities that make us beautifully human. As we navigate the tender terrain of self-reflection, may we approach each query with an open heart, recognizing the strength that arises from embracing our truth. This introspective voyage is an opportunity to cultivate a garden of self-compassion and unveil the richness that resides within.

You gain strength, courage, and confidence by every
experience in which you really stop to look fear in the face.
You are able to say to yourself, 'I lived through this horror.
I can take the next thing that comes along.

- Eleanor Roosevelt

Self-Reflection: A Brave Journey Within

In the sanctuary of self-reflection, we embark on a courageous expedition into the depths of our hearts, acknowledging the challenges that may arise like gentle waves. Each question is a lantern illuminating the corridors of our inner landscapes. Let us navigate this sacred space with tenderness and an open heart.

To truly immerse yourself in this process, we encourage you to answer just one question each day. Make this practice a part of your daily routine, filling your journal over time. The depth of the questions posed warrants your full attention and introspection for an entire day. Attempting to answer multiple questions in one sitting may dilute the experience and make it less impactful.

Your journey begins now. Welcome to the fascinating adventure of knowing yourself more profoundly than ever before. Here's to your journey of self-discovery and to the incredible insights that await you!

Best of luck on this transformative journey. May each page turned and every question answered bring you closer to understanding your true self, fostering growth and awakening within.

Write up something you can't talk about:

What makes loving you difficult?

What's on your mind that's
messing with your sleep?

Are you the one causing your own problems? How?

Do you remember the last time
you were sincerely happy?

What are those things you can't tell your parents?

What were those words that broke you inside?

When was the last time
someone made you feel loved?

When was the first time you let someone
see your true self and ended up feeling rejected?

What would you say to your parents if you could write them an anonymous letter telling them everything you think they have done wrong?

Do you like who you are?

Write about your worst traumas.

Write about your first heartbreak.

What would you do if there
was nothing holding you back?

What was the worst thing
you ever did to yourself?

What is your real dream?

Which group of people are you most focused
on pleasing or impressing? Is it healthy?

When do you think you felt
most like yourself in your life?

What is a self-promise that you have
broken and still keep breaking, and why?

What is the worst act you have
ever committed? What drove you to it?
Have you ever discussed it with anyone?

What is the one thing someone might
say to you to make you fall to your knees?
Why do such words have such a strong impact?

Be truthful with yourself.
Do you genuinely believe that your
life is going in the right direction?

Do you feel that you only experience
love during good or successful times?

What are the words that would console you?

Is there something bothering you
that you want to open up about?

Do you have any unresolved issues from
the past that you're unable to release? If so, why?

Can you tell me about the most
difficult farewell you've experienced?

Share those moments when you did cool stuff your parents didn't notice. You totally deserved some props.

Who is there for you, making you feel loved
when you're struggling to feel that way?

Is there a recurring thought that
keeps you awake at night?

Are you sabotaging your own
growth or happiness? How?

Describe a moment when
words shattered your inner peace.

Write about the most challenging
experiences you've endured.

Describe the most self-destructive action you've taken and its underlying reasons.

Have you ever felt like you're
living a life that's not truly your own?

When was the last time you
doubted your own abilities or worth?

Describe a time when you had to stand up for your beliefs or values.

Write about a situation that
challenged your sense of identity.

Have you ever felt like you're living
according to someone else's expectations?

What's the most significant life lesson you've learned so far, and how did it impact you?

Ever feel like you're just going through the motions?

Do you remember any acts of
kindness from strangers that touched you?

What's your relationship with time like?
Feel rushed or pretty chill?

Is there a special place that means a lot to you?
What's the story?

Do you think that social networks
are helping you in your life? Why?

Have your parents ever told you that they are proud of you? How did you feel?

What are the top three values
that guide your life choices?

Is there any phrase or saying that you always keep in mind in your life?

Who is the person that inspires
you the most, and why?

What's the best piece of advice you've ever received, and how did it impact you?

What do you believe is the key to
maintaining a healthy work-life balance?

What's your approach to dealing
with setbacks and failures in life?

Can you identify a personal achievement that made you feel genuinely proud of yourself?

Share a story about a time when you overcame a personal limitation or fear.

Who does your heart feel safest with?

What would you do if success was guaranteed?

Chapter 6: The Healing Power of Mindfulness

Dearest reader, as we step into the nurturing embrace of Chapter 6, we delve into the profound realm where mindfulness becomes a healing balm for our emotional well-being. Like a gentle stream that soothes the wounds of the heart, mindfulness holds the transformative power to mend and restore. In the following pages, we will explore the profound connection between mindfulness and emotional healing, sharing stories that illuminate the journey of those who found solace in its gentle embrace. Within these lines, you'll discover exercises crafted with care, designed to guide you on a path of emotional balance and inner harmony.

The Dance of Mindfulness and Emotional Well-being: A Symphony of Healing

Mindfulness is not merely a practice; it is a tender companion on our journey toward emotional equilibrium. In this chapter, we will unravel the threads that connect mindfulness and the healing of emotional wounds. The mindfulness journey is one of self-discovery, where we learn to hold our emotions with kindness, acknowledging their presence without judgment.

Stories of Healing: Whispers of Resilience

Let me share with you the stories of Emily and James, two souls whose paths were transformed through the healing power of mindfulness.

Emily's Journey to Inner Calm:
Emily, burdened by the weight of anxiety, discovered solace in mindful breathing. With each intentional breath, she learned to release the grip of worry, creating space for tranquility to blossom. Through consistent practice, Emily cultivated a sanctuary of peace within, navigating life's storms with newfound resilience.

James's Transformation through Mindful Presence:
James, haunted by the ghosts of past traumas, found refuge in the present moment. Through mindfulness meditation, he learned to anchor himself in the now, untethering from the shadows that haunted his past. The healing journey wasn't instantaneous, but with each mindful breath, James embraced the light of the present, fostering a gradual healing of the soul.

These stories are testaments to the transformative potential of mindfulness. They remind us that within the cocoon of mindfulness, wounds can heal, and emotional scars can transform into badges of resilience.

Exercises for Emotional Healing: A Gentle Guide to Balance

1. Mindful Breathing for Calm:
Find a quiet space and take a few moments to focus on your breath. Inhale deeply, feeling the air fill your lungs, and exhale slowly, releasing tension. With each breath, visualize a wave of calm washing over you.

2. Loving-Kindness Meditation:
Close your eyes and, with a compassionate heart, repeat phrases like "May I be happy, may I be healthy, may I be safe, may I be at ease." Extend these wishes to yourself and gradually to others. Feel the warmth of loving-kindness enveloping your being.

3. Emotional Body Scan:
Sit or lie down comfortably and bring your awareness to different parts of your body. Notice any areas of tension or discomfort. With each breath, imagine sending soothing energy to these areas, allowing them to release and relax.

4. Mindful Journaling:
Set aside time to reflect on your emotions. Write without judgment,

allowing your thoughts and feelings to flow onto the pages. This practice fosters self-awareness and provides a safe space for emotional expression.

5. Nature Connection:

Spend time in nature, whether it's a park, garden, or a quiet corner of your neighborhood. Engage your senses—feel the earth beneath you, listen to the rustle of leaves, and breathe in the fresh air. Nature has a profound healing presence that can bring a sense of peace.

Dear reader, as you embark on the path of emotional healing through mindfulness, may you approach each exercise with the gentle touch of self-compassion. Within the sanctuary of your heart, let mindfulness be the healer, stitching together the fragments of your emotional landscape. As you tread this path, may you discover the resilience within, emerging from the cocoon of mindfulness with wings of newfound strength and balance.

Goal Setting: Nurturing the Seeds of Personal Aspirations

In this sacred corner of the "Healing" journal, let us embark on a journey of self-discovery and empowerment through the art of goal setting. The canvas of your life awaits the strokes of your aspirations, both short and long term, creating a roadmap toward a future shaped by your dreams. In the following pages, we will cultivate a garden of intentionality, guiding you to articulate, plan, and celebrate the milestones on your path to personal growth.

Short and Long Term Goals: A Tapestry of Aspirations

Begin this section by defining the dreams that reside within your heart. Whether they unfold in the rhythm of weeks, months, or span across years, let these goals be specific, realistic, and a true reflection of your deepest desires. Like stars guiding your journey, each goal is a beacon illuminating the path to your aspirations.

Step Planning: Unveiling the Blueprint of Achievement

Seemingly towering goals become manageable with the magic of step planning. Break down each goal into smaller, achievable tasks. Like a sculptor chiseling away excess stone to reveal the masterpiece within, step planning transforms the abstract into the tangible, allowing you to witness the birth of your accomplishments.

Deadline: Infusing Time with Purpose

Set realistic deadlines as companions on your journey. Each deadline becomes a waypoint, infusing your goals with a sense of urgency and purpose. These temporal markers not only guide your progress but also provide the rhythm to your dance of achievement.

Progress Tracking: A Mirror to Your Journey

In the quiet corners of this section, create a haven for progress tracking. Witness the evolution of your endeavors, acknowledging the steps taken and the distance yet to be traversed. This reflective space empowers you to adjust your sails as needed, ensuring that your journey aligns with the vision you've crafted.

Rewards and Celebrations: Honoring Your Triumphs

As you inch closer to your goals, conjure visions of rewards and celebrations. These are not mere indulgences but tokens of acknowledgment for your resilience and dedication. Let them serve as beacons of joy, encouraging you to persevere on the path you've paved.

Goals in Different Areas of Life: Balancing the Symphony of Aspirations

Diversify the garden of your goals across various facets of life. Plant seeds in the soil of career, education, relationships, physical and emotional well-being, and personal growth. Each area is a petal contributing to the vibrant bloom of your holistic journey.

Motivational Reminders: Echoes of Empowerment

Embrace the power of motivational reminders—inspirational quotes and affirmations that resonate with your spirit. Let these words be the melody that accompanies you, uplifting your soul when challenges arise and bolstering your resolve as you chase your dreams.

Periodic Review: Nurturing the Ever-Growing Garden

Periodically, sit amidst the blossoms of your goals and review their petals. Adjust the plan if the winds of life sway you in unexpected directions, and fear not to set new goals as you evolve on this journey of personal growth. The periodic review is a dance of adaptation, ensuring that your goals align with the rhythm of your evolving self.

In this section, young readers are equipped with a profound tool—a compass that not only guides them through the landscape of their aspirations but also nurtures the seeds of self-discovery and empowerment. With each stroke of intentionality, may you sculpt a masterpiece that reflects the strength and beauty within.

Owning our story and loving ourselves through that process is the bravest thing that we'll ever do.

- Brené Brown

Chapter 7: Mindful Connections in Relationships

Fellow explorer, welcome to the heart of mindful connections—a sacred space where the threads of mindfulness weave a tapestry of meaningful relationships. In this chapter, we explore the profound role of mindfulness in fostering connections that resonate with depth and authenticity. As your companion on this journey, I offer gentle guidance on infusing mindfulness into the fabric of your relationships, creating spaces where understanding, empathy, and love flourish. Within these pages, you'll find personal stories that illuminate how mindfulness, like a gentle breeze, has enriched the soil of my own connections, allowing them to bloom with compassion.

The Dance of Mindfulness in Relationships: A Symphony of Connection

Mindfulness is the gentle whisper that transforms the ordinary into the extraordinary, and nowhere is its magic more palpable than in the realm of relationships. In this chapter, we'll unravel the layers of mindfulness, exploring how it becomes the silent architect of meaningful connections. Let us embark on this journey with open hearts, ready to embrace the transformative power of mindful connections.

Guidance on Bringing Mindfulness into Relationships: Nurturing the Roots of Connection

1. Present Moment Awareness:

Encourage yourself and your loved ones to be fully present in each moment. Whether it's a shared meal, a conversation, or a simple touch, savor the richness of the present moment together.

2. Deep Listening:

Cultivate the art of deep listening, allowing each word to be a note in the melody of your connection. Let go of the urge to respond immediately, and instead, listen with the intention to understand.

3. Non-Judgmental Acceptance:

Create a space free of judgment, where each person can express themselves authentically. Embrace the uniqueness of your loved ones, appreciating the beauty in their individuality.

4. Empathy in Action:

Practice empathy as a language of the heart. Step into the shoes of your loved ones, feeling the contours of their emotions. Let empathy be the bridge that connects your souls.

5. Mindful Communication:

Foster mindful communication by expressing yourself with clarity and kindness. Before responding in moments of tension, take a breath and choose words that build bridges rather than walls.

6. Cultivating Gratitude:

Infuse your relationships with gratitude. Take moments to express appreciation for the small and big things, recognizing the beauty that each person brings to your life.

Personal Stories of Enriched Connections:
Whispers of Shared Mindfulness

Allow me to share glimpses of my own journey with mindfulness in relationships:

The Art of Presence:
In a quiet moment with a dear friend, we found connection not in grand gestures, but in the simple act of being present. Mindfulness became our shared language, creating a space where time seemed to slow down, and our hearts spoke volumes.

Transformative Power of Listening:
In a conversation with a loved one during challenging times, the

practice of deep listening became a balm for both our souls. Through mindful presence and listening, we discovered the strength to navigate the storms together, emerging with a deeper bond.

These stories are testament to the alchemy that unfolds when mindfulness becomes the foundation of relationships. Like a gentle current guiding a river, mindfulness shapes the contours of connections, infusing them with depth, understanding, and a shared sense of presence.

Dear reader, may this chapter be a lantern guiding you toward mindful connections. As you weave the threads of mindfulness into the fabric of your relationships, may you discover a tapestry of love, understanding, and shared moments that resonate with authenticity.

Understanding someone's suffering is the best gift you can give another person. Understanding is love's other name. If you don't understand, you can't love.

- Thích Nhất Hạnh

Chapter 8: Mindfulness Across Lifetimes

Hello, fellow seeker, as we delve into the final chapters of our mindful journey, we find ourselves at the crossroads of ages—a place where the gentle embrace of mindfulness transcends generations. In this chapter, we unravel the profound benefits of introducing mindfulness to both the youngest and wisest among us. With an open heart and the spirit of a caring guide, I invite you to explore age-appropriate mindfulness exercises tailored for different life stages. Within these pages, you'll discover touching stories that illuminate the intergenerational dance of mindfulness, weaving a tapestry of connection and shared presence.

The Timeless Benefits of Mindfulness: Nurturing Souls Across Lifetimes

Mindfulness is a gift that knows no bounds—it is a timeless practice that nourishes both the budding innocence of childhood and the seasoned wisdom of older adulthood. In this chapter, we celebrate the ageless beauty of mindfulness, acknowledging its transformative power at every stage of life.

Benefits of Mindfulness for Children:

Planting Seeds of Presence

1. Emotional Regulation:

Mindfulness becomes a gentle guide for children to navigate the vast landscape of their emotions. Through simple practices, they learn to identify, understand, and express their feelings with grace.

2. Concentration and Focus:

In a world filled with distractions, mindfulness becomes a beacon that cultivates the ability to focus. Through playful exercises, children develop concentration skills that serve them in both learning and play.

3. Building Resilience:

Mindfulness becomes a protective cloak, shielding children from the storms of life. By teaching them to be present in the face of challenges, we nurture resilience that will accompany them into adulthood.

Mindfulness for Older Adults:

Embracing the Wisdom of the Ages

1. Promoting Cognitive Well-being:

Mindfulness becomes a fountain of youth for the mind, promoting cognitive well-being in older adults. Through practices that engage the senses, they can savor the richness of each moment, fostering mental clarity and acuity.

2. Enhancing Emotional Balance:

In the tapestry of aging, mindfulness becomes a thread that enhances emotional balance. Through practices that embrace self-compassion and acceptance, older adults find solace in the present, releasing the weight of the past.

3. Connecting Across Generations:

Mindfulness becomes a bridge that spans generations. Through shared practices, older adults and the younger members of their families create bonds woven with the threads of presence, understanding, and love.

Touching Stories of Intergenerational Mindfulness: A Symphony of Connection

Let me share with you stories that resonate with the gentle echoes of intergenerational mindfulness:

Grandmother's Guiding Breath:

In the stillness of the morning, a grandmother and her grandchild found connection through the simple act of mindful breathing. As they sat together, inhaling and exhaling, they discovered a language that transcended words—an unspoken bond that wove through the generations.

Playful Moments with Mindful Games:

In a bustling family gathering, mindfulness became a playful adventure. Children and older adults engaged in age-appropriate mindfulness games, fostering laughter and shared joy. These moments became the threads that stitched together the fabric of familial connection.

These stories illuminate the transformative power of mindfulness across lifetimes. Whether in the boundless curiosity of childhood or the reflective wisdom of older adulthood, mindfulness serves as a companion, guiding each soul toward a deeper connection with the present.

Dear reader, as you explore the ageless realms of mindfulness, may you find inspiration in these stories and discover the timeless beauty of shared presence. In every breath, at every stage of life, may mindfulness be a gentle guide, nurturing your soul with the wisdom of the ages.

Your visions will become clear only when you can look into your own heart. Who looks outside, dreams; who looks inside, awakes.

- Carl Jung

Chapter 9: Creating Your Sacred Space

Dearest reader, as we near the culmination of our mindful journey, we find ourselves at the threshold of a sanctuary—a space where the external world harmonizes with the internal realm, creating the perfect environment for mindfulness to flourish. In this chapter, we delve into the importance of cultivating a nurturing environment, offering you gentle tips to create a personal sacred space for your practice. As a caring guide, I share insights on how the ambiance around you intertwines with your well-being, shaping the tapestry of your mindful journey.

The Harmony of Environment and Mindfulness: Nurturing Your Inner Garden

The world around us is a symphony of energies that can either uplift or diminish our spirit. Recognizing the significance of environment in the practice of mindfulness, we embark on a journey to create a sacred space—a cocoon of tranquility where the echoes of your breath harmonize with the cadence of your heart.

Tips on Creating Your Personal Sacred Space: Crafting a Haven for Mindfulness

1. Choose a Quiet Corner:

Identify a quiet corner in your home or a serene outdoor spot where you can retreat from the demands of daily life. Let this space be a sanctuary that beckons you to stillness.

2. Infuse Nature's Presence:

Bring a touch of nature into your sacred space. Whether it's a potted plant, a vase of flowers, or a view of the outdoors, nature has a transformative power to ground and center your being.

3. Soft Lighting and Comfortable Seating:

Illuminate your space with soft, soothing lighting. Opt for natural light during the day and warm, gentle lighting in the evening. Choose comfortable seating that supports a relaxed yet attentive posture.

4. Create an Altar or Focal Point:

Craft an altar or designate a focal point that holds personal significance. This could be a candle, a piece of artwork, or a cherished item that evokes a sense of peace and connection.

5. Include Mindful Symbols:

Integrate symbols of mindfulness into your space, such as a meditation cushion, a singing bowl, or a representation of a calming mantra. These objects serve as reminders of your intention to be present.

6. Aromatherapy and Soundscapes:

Engage the senses through aromatherapy and soothing sounds. Choose essential oils that promote relaxation and play gentle background music or nature sounds to create a harmonious atmosphere.

Insights on the Impact of Environment on Well-being: A Tapestry of Connection

The environment we inhabit is not merely a backdrop to our lives; it is an active participant in our well-being. As you create your sacred space for mindfulness, consider the profound impact it can have on your inner landscape.

A Calm Haven for the Soul:

Your sacred space becomes a haven where the external chaos dissipates, allowing the soul to find respite. In this tranquil oasis, the mind unwinds, and the heart opens to the beauty of the present moment.

The Alchemy of Atmosphere:

The ambiance you craft shapes the atmosphere of your mindful practice. A space infused with serenity and intention becomes a fertile ground where mindfulness takes root and blossoms.

Connection Between Outer and Inner Worlds:

The external environment mirrors the internal landscape of your mind. As you cultivate a nurturing space, you cultivate a relationship with the self, fostering a sense of balance and inner harmony.

Dear reader, may this chapter guide you in creating a sacred space that resonates with the melody of your heart. As you infuse intention into the ambiance around you, may you discover that the sanctuary you create becomes a reflection of the peace you seek within.

Motivating Phrases: Nurturing Your Mindful Haven

Within the sacred space of mindfulness, let these motivating phrases become the gentle breeze that stirs the leaves of your inner garden. As you craft your personal sanctuary, let these words resonate, inspiring you to infuse your space with the essence of positivity, healing, and self-love.

I see the best of me when I'm with you.

It's not what I feel for you;

it's what I don't feel for anyone but you.

It's important to find people who make
you realize there's nothing wrong with
being who you are.

Why are you still holding on?

Stop playing out painful scenarios in your mind that don't exist in the present.

Are you ready for the
love you say you want?

If you feel like giving up right now,
please keep going. You're so close
but you can't see it from where
you are right now.

Growing sometimes means

leaving people behind.

Glad we met. I hope you
stay around for a long time.

I know I met you for a reason.

Meeting you was a nice accident.

You feel like home today.

Forgive yourself like you
did your ex so many times.

It's okay if it still hurts.

I think it ended right when it needed to.

Thank yourself for how far you've come.

You'll get over it just like
you got over that other thing.

It's okay to still cry over things
you thought you moved past.

It's okay if you're still hurting over
something you thought you'd healed
from. It's okay if your progress
seems backward or feels slow.
It's okay if you've still got
some healing to do.

I hope you know how special you are.

Stop going back to people
who keep hurting you.

Thank people for the small things
they do that make you feel loved.

Stop being shocked by
repeated behavior.

One honest conversation
can change everything.

You're so in your head you can't
even enjoy where you are.

Every version of you
deserves to be loved.

There's nothing wrong with walking

away from something that's

no longer serving you.

You don't need to have it all figured out.
You just need to be doing something
that makes you happy.

Sometimes good things end
because people aren't ready.

They'll remember the feeling
you leave with them.

Your anxiety is lying to you.

Don't spend another year
doing the same thing.

Put yourself first and don't

fucking apologize for it.

No one is you, and that is your power.

Don't let your fear decide your future.

Rule number 1:

Fuck what they think.

Note to self: I'm going to
make you so damn proud.

They're going to judge anyway,

so whatever.

Shit happens. Move on.

You deserve better. You know you do.

Don't lose this moment
searching for another.

Take more chances, dance more dances.

Be human to the fullest.

I'll be the kid with big plans.

Don't be jealous of people;
be inspired.

Doubt kills more dreams
than failure ever will.

I know you are scared,
but you can handle this.

You don't miss the person;

you miss the feeling.

A negative mind will
never give you a positive life.

Chapter 10: Embracing Mindfulness in the Digital Era

As we bring this journey of mindfulness to a close, let's delve into a realm that many of us navigate daily—the digital landscape. In a world where screens illuminate our lives, where the constant hum of notifications can drown out the whispers of tranquility, finding mindfulness in the digital age becomes a poignant quest.

Finding Serenity in the Digital Buzz

In this chapter, we embark on a quest to harmonize our relationship with technology, recognizing that screens need not be barriers to peace but gateways to serenity. The stories shared here are not just anecdotes; they are beacons guiding us through the labyrinth of the digital world.

Celebrities Embracing Digital Mindfulness

Discover how celebrities, amidst the whirlwind of fame and digital connectivity, weave threads of mindfulness into the fabric of their daily lives. From managing social media usage to incorporating mindful practices into their tech routines, these figures illuminate a path toward a balanced coexistence with the digital age.

Practical Tips for Digital Serenity

As we navigate this era of constant connectivity, let's uncover practical tips and heartfelt advice on infusing mindfulness into our digital interactions. From mindful app usage to creating digital sanctuaries, we'll explore how technology can become a conduit for calm rather than chaos.

Virtual Journeys to Inner Peace

Explore the emergence of meditation apps, virtual well-being experiences, and online communities fostering mindful connections. In this chapter, we embrace the idea that, in the digital realm, there exists a vast landscape of opportunities to cultivate inner peace and strengthen our connection to the present moment.

Here are a few examples of celebrities who have embraced digital mindfulness in various ways:

1. Ashton Kutcher:

  - Ashton Kutcher has been vocal about the importance of digital detoxes. He, along with his wife Mila Kunis, takes regular breaks from social media and technology to spend quality time with family and be present in the moment.

2. Arianna Huffington:

- The co-founder of The Huffington Post, Arianna Huffington, is a strong advocate for digital well-being. She emphasizes the need for a healthy relationship with technology and even created the "Thrive" app, which encourages users to unplug and recharge.

3. Emma Stone:

- Emma Stone has spoken about her decision to avoid social media to protect her mental health. By opting out of the constant digital chatter, she maintains a mindful approach to her personal well-being.

4. Keanu Reeves:

- Keanu Reeves, known for his roles in iconic films, is not active on social media. He values his privacy and prefers to keep a distance from the digital noise, showcasing a mindful approach to managing his public image.

5. Gwyneth Paltrow:

- Gwyneth Paltrow, founder of Goop, has advocated for mindful technology use, especially when it comes to parenting. She promotes setting boundaries and creating tech-free zones to foster meaningful connections within families.

6. Russell Brand:

- Comedian and actor Russell Brand has openly discussed his decision to step away from social media. He believes in the importance of maintaining mental clarity and avoiding the potential pitfalls of constant digital engagement.

These celebrities demonstrate that digital mindfulness is a personal choice, and each individual can find a balance that aligns with their well-being goals.

A Supportive Invitation

Dear reader, as you step forward into the digital mindfulness age, consider this chapter a supportive invitation. Let these insights be a comforting companion as you navigate the screens that surround you. May your digital interactions become a mindful dance, a harmonious melody in the symphony of your well-being.

Technology is nothing. What's important is that you have a faith in people, that they're basically good and smart, and if you give them tools, they'll do wonderful things with them.

- Steve Jobs

Conclusion:
A Compassionate
Journey

As we draw the curtains on our shared odyssey of mindfulness and self-discovery, I extend my heartfelt gratitude for embarking on this compassionate journey with me. Together, we have explored the depths of mindfulness, uncovering the transformative power it holds for cultivating inner peace and self-love.

In our pursuit of mindfulness, we have:

1. Nurtured the Inner Garden:

- We planted seeds of awareness and tended to the blooms of compassion, creating a sanctuary within our hearts where tranquility reigns.

2. Breathed in the Gentle Power:

- With each mindful breath, we harnessed the quiet strength within, embracing the transformative power of simply being present.

3. Cultivated Self-Compassion:

- Through gentle exercises and reflections, we sowed the seeds of self-compassion, allowing ourselves to flourish in the warmth of kindness.

4. Embraced the Present Moment:

- In the beauty of the present moment, we discovered joy in the simplicity of daily life, savoring each experience with a heart full of gratitude.

5. Navigated Challenges with Grace:

   - Acknowledging the challenges, we faced them with grace and compassion, recognizing that each obstacle is an opportunity for growth.

6. Experienced the Healing Power of Mindfulness:

   - Our journey delved into the healing embrace of mindfulness, witnessing stories of emotional restoration and balance.

7. Fostered Mindful Connections:

   - We explored the profound role mindfulness plays in relationships, recognizing that meaningful connections bloom in the soil of presence.

8. Embraced Mindfulness Across Lifetimes:

   - From the youngest hearts to the wisest souls, we uncovered the universal benefits of mindfulness, transcending generations with stories that touched our spirits.

9. Created Your Sacred Space:

   - In crafting your sacred space, you cultivated a haven infused with motivation, healing, and the unwavering support of self-love.

As this book gently closes, remember that your journey with mindfulness is an ongoing expedition, a continual blossoming of self-awareness and compassion. You now hold the keys to a mindful life, where each step is a dance, each breath a melody, and each moment an opportunity for presence.

I express my deepest gratitude for your commitment to this journey. Your dedication to mindfulness is a gift to yourself, echoing the love and care you deserve. As you continue forward, may the path be sprinkled with moments of peace, joy, and profound self-discovery.

Remember, dear reader, you are not alone. The wisdom of mindfulness is always within reach, guiding you through the ebb and flow of life's journey. Should you ever need a companion on this path, know that the support and encouragement found within these pages are everlasting.

Printed in Poland
by Amazon Fulfillment
Poland Sp. z o.o., Wrocław

31487323R00107